# MICR

F

# BBC



**Professor Peter Morse**
**Brian Hancock**

GUILD PUBLISHING LONDON

## CONTENTS


| | | |
|---|---|---|
| 1 | Keys and Cursors | 3 |
| 2 | BASIC Keywords (alphabetical list of all commands) | 5 |
| | 2.1 Operating commands | 8 |
| | 2.2 General commands | 9 |
| | 2.3 Graphics, text and colour | 14 |
| | 2.4 Sound | 19 |
| | 2.5 Numeric and Trigonometric Functions | 20 |
| | 2.6 Input/Output Instructions | 22 |
| | 2.7 String Functions | 25 |
| | 2.8 Arithmetic and Logic Operations | 26 |
| | 2.9 File-handling commands | 28 |
| | 2.10 Memory and machine code commands | 30 |
| | 2.11 Error handling | 32 |
| 3 | Error Messages | 32 |
| 4 | Memory map and memory map assignments | 36 |
| 5 | Operating System commands | 37 |
| 6 | Operating System calls | 38 |
| 7 | FX and OSBYTE call summary | 38 |
| 8 | Disc Operating System commands | 40 |
| 9 | ASCII codes and Key values | 42 |

# 1 KEYS AND CURSORS

■ white square cursor WRITE cursor
– flashing line cursor READ cursor

Normal use **CAPS LOCK** on **SHIFT LOCK** off

Cursor control keys ← → ↑ ↓

**DELETE**
Erases last character typed on screen.

**COPY**
Used in conjunction with cursor control key to edit program.

**ESCAPE**
*First abort key* stops running program.

**BREAK**
*Second abort key* stops computer whatever it is doing. *Soft reset*, does not affect clock or user-defined keys.

**CTRL BREAK**
*Hard reset.* Resets everything.

**CTRL**
Pressed with another key performs some operation. [see VDU summary]

**RETURN**
Causes command to be acted upon.

**SHIFT**
Produces symbol on top of key etc. Also turns page in paging mode.

**TAB**
Moves WRITE cursor one position to the right.

**SHIFT CTRL**
Stops scrolling.

**SHIFT BREAK**
Used to autoboot with special program.

**USER DEFINED KEYS**
Keys at top of keyboard, labelled $f_1$, $f_2$, ... $f_0$, can be used to generate any string of characters.

Example:
*KEY 3 MODE 6 ¦ M ¦ N LIST ¦ M **RETURN** will produce on pressing **f3** a listing of a program in MODE 6 with paging.

* passes control to operating system.

KEY 3 specifies key.

¦ M represents **RETURN** (i.e CTRL M).

¦ N enters paging mode (i.e CTRL N).

LIST lists program.

¦ M represents **RETURN**

Can also use **BREAK**, **COPY**, ←, →, ↓, ↑ as user defined keys 10 to 15 respectively.
A soft break does *not* clear definitions but a hard break does (see above).

CONVENTIONS

**n, m, p**
Numeric expressions

**S**
String expression

**X, Y**
Co-ordinates (numbers)

**NV, SV, V**
Numeric variable, string variable, variable

< >
Statement

**[ ]**
Optional items

SECTIONS

1 Operating commands
2 General instructions
3 Graphics and Colour
4 Sound
5 Numeric and trigonometrical functions
6 Input/Output Instructions
7 String functions
8 Arithmetic and Logical Operations
9 File-handling
10 Memory and machine code
11 Error Handling

# 2 BASIC KEYWORDS

**Minimum abbreviation never needs an opening bracket*

| Keyword | Brief meaning | *Min abbr | Section |
|---|---|---|---|
| ABS | absolute value | ABS | 5 |
| ACS | arc-cosine | ACS | 5 |
| ADVAL | analogue to digital converter value | AD. | 10 |
| AND | logical and (bitwise and) | A. | 8 |
| ASC | American Standard Code | ASC | 7 |
| ASN | arc-sine | ASN | 5 |
| ATN | arc-tangent | ATN | 5 |
| AUTO | automatic line generator | AU. | 1 |
| BGET # | gets byte from file | B.# | 9 |
| BPUT # | puts byte into file | BP.# | 9 |
| CALL | calls machine code routine | CA. | 10 |
| CHAIN | chain program | CH. | 1 |
| CHR$ | character string | CHR. | 7 |
| CLEAR | clear variables | CL. | 1 |
| CLOSE # | closes file | CLO.# | 9 |
| CLG | clears graphics screen | CLG | 3 |
| CLS | clears text screen | CLS | 3 |
| COLOUR | selects text colour | C. | 3 |
| COS | cosine | COS | 5 |
| COUNT | counts characters | COU. | 6 |
| DATA | data | D. | 2 |
| DEF | define function or procedure | DEF | 2 |
| DEG | degrees | DEG | 5 |
| DELETE | deletes lines from program | DEL. | 1 |
| DIM | dimensions array | DIM | 2 |
| DIV | division of integers | DIV | 5 |
| DRAW | draws line | DR. | 3 |
| ELSE | else | EL. | 2 |
| END | end of program | END | 2 |
| ENDPROC | end of procedure | E. | 2 |
| ENVELOPE | envelope of sound | ENV. | 4 |
| EOF # | end of file test | EOF # | 9 |
| EOR | exclusive or (bitwise exclusive or) | EOR | 8 |
| ERL | error line number | ERL | 11 |
| ERR | error | ERR | 11 |
| ERROR | suppress error message | ERR. | 11 |
| EVAL | evaluate expression | EV. | 2 |
| EXP | exponential | EXP | 5 |
| EXT # | extent of file | EXT # | 9 |
| FALSE | false | FA. | 8 |
| FN | function | FN | 2 |
| FOR | for loop | F. | 2 |
| GCOL | sets graphics colour | GC. | 3 |

| Keyword | Brief meaning | *Min abbr | Section |
|---|---|---|---|
| FN | function | FN | 2 |
| FOR | for loop | F. | 2 |
| GCOL | sets graphics colour | GC. | 3 |
| GET | get ASCII value of key pressed | GET | 6 |
| GET$ | get character of key pressed | GE. | 6 |
| GOSUB | go to subroutine | GOS. | 2 |
| GOTO | go to line | G. | 2 |
| HIMEM | highest memory | H. | 10 |
| IF | if | IF | 2 |
| INKEY | gives ASCII value of key pressed | INKEY | 6 |
| INKEY$ | gives character of key pressed | INK. | 6 |
| INPUT | inputs data | I. | 6 |
| INPUT# | inputs information from file | I.# | 9 |
| INSTR | in string | INS. | 7 |
| INT | integer | INT | 5 |
| LEFT$ | left string | LE. | 7 |
| LEN | length of string | LEN | 7 |
| LET | let | LET | 2 |
| LIST | lists program | L. | 1 |
| LISTO | list option | L.O | 1 |
| LN | natural logarithm | LN | 5 |
| LOAD | loads program | LO. | 1 |
| LOCAL | local variables | LOC. | 2 |
| LOG | logarithm | LOG | 5 |
| LOMEM | lowest memory | LOM. | 10 |
| MID$ | middle of string | M. | 7 |
| MOD | modulus | MOD | 5 |
| MODE | graphics mode | MO. | 3 |
| MOVE | move graphics cursor | MOV. | 3 |
| NEW | new program | NEW | 1 |
| NEXT | next | N. | 2 |
| NOT | logical inverse | NOT | 8 |
| OLD | recovers old program | O. | 1 |
| ON | on | ON | 2 |
| OPENIN | open file for input | OP. | 9 |
| OPENOUT | open file for output | OPENO. | 9 |
| OPENUP | opens file | OPENU. | 9 |
| OPT | option | OPT | 10 |
| OR | logical or (bitwise or) | OR | 8 |
| OSCL1 | operating system command line interpreter pass BASIC | OS. | 10 |
| PAGE | address of BASIC program | PA. | 10 |
| PI | pi ($\pi$) | PI | 5 |
| PLOT | plot drawing | PL. | 3 |
| POINT | point colour | PO. | 3 |

| Keyword | Brief meaning | *Min abbr | Section |
|---|---|---|---|
| POS | horizontal position of cursor | POS | 3 |
| PRINT | prints to screen | P. | 6 |
| PRINT# | writes to file | P.# | 9 |
| PROC | procedure | PRO. | 2 |
| PTR# | reserved for future use | PT# | 9 |
| RAD | radians | RAD | 5 |
| READ | read data | REA. | 2 |
| REM | remark | REM | 2 |
| RENUMBER | renumber program lines | REN. | 1 |
| REPEAT | repeat loop | REP. | 2 |
| REPORT | report error message | REPO. | 11 |
| RESTORE | restore data pointer | RES. | 2 |
| RETURN | return from subroutine | R. | 2 |
| RIGHT$ | right string | RI. | 7 |
| RND | random number | RND | 5 |
| RUN | runs program | * | 1 |
| SAVE | saves program | SA. | 1 |
| SGN | signum (sign) | SGN | 5 |
| SIN | sine | SIN | 5 |
| SOUND | sound | SO. | 4 |
| SPC | space | SPC | 6 |
| SQR | square root function | SQR | 5 |
| STEP | step | S. | 2 |
| STOP | stops execution | STO. | 2 |
| STR$ | string representation | STR. | 7 |
| STRING$ | multiple strings | STRI. | 7 |
| TAB | tabulation | TAB | 6 |
| TAN | tangent | T. | 5 |
| THEN | then | TH. | 2 |
| TIME | time | TI. | 2 |
| TO | to | TO | 2 |
| TOP | top of memory | TOP | 10 |
| TRACE | traces execution | TR. | 11 |
| TRUE | true | TRUE | 8 |
| UNTIL | until | U. | 2 |
| USR | user | USR | 10 |
| VAL | value – function | VAL | 7 |
| VDU | VDU | V. | 3 |
| VPOS | vertical position of cursor | VP. | 3 |
| WIDTH | width of page | W. | 6 |
| : | statement separator | : | 2 |
| ? | byte indirection operator | ? | 10 |
| ! | word indirection operator | ! | 10 |
| $ | string (or string indirection operator) | $ | 7(10) |
| & | hexadecimal number | & | 10 |
| @% | PRINT format | @% | 6 |
| ∧ (or ↑) | exponentiation | ∧ (or ↑) | 8 |

## 2.1 OPERATING COMMANDS

**AUTO [n, m]**
Automatically generates line numbers starting at line n with m the increment between line numbers. Leave AUTO mode using ESCAPE. Default value for n and m is 10.
Example: AUTO 100 generates lines numbers 100, 110, 120...

**CHAIN s**
Enables the program specified to be LOADed and RUN automatically.
Example: CHAIN "PROG"

**CLEAR**
Clears all variables except resident integer variables.

**DELETE n, m**
Deletes a group of lines from program where n is first line deleted and m last line deleted.
Example: DELETE 100, 500 deletes lines between 100 and 500 inclusive

**LIST [n, m]**
Produces a listing of the program between lines n and m inclusive. Default on n is first line and on m the last line of program.
Examples:
LIST 200, 500 lists lines 200 to 500 inclusive.
LIST lists the whole program.
LIST 350 lists the single line 350.
LIST 200, lists lines 200 onward.
LIST , 1000 lists lines up to line 1000.

**LISTO n**
Provides an indented listing of a program
n = 0 no inserted spaces
n = 1 space after line number
n = 2 spaces during FOR... NEXT loops
n = 4 spaces during REPEAT... UNTIL loops
Example: LISTO7 puts spaces after line numbers, double spaces for FOR... NEXT and REPEAT .... UNTIL loops.

**LOAD s**
Loads program s from current file system (tape, disc or network).
Examples: LOAD "FILNAM" loads program named FILNAM.
LOAD " " loads the next program from tape but does *not* work on disc or network.

**NEW**
Removes program from memory. Use before entering a new program [see OLD]

**OLD**
Recovers a program which has just been removed by NEW or BREAK. Only works if no new program lines or variables have been entered since program was deleted.

**RENUMBER [n, m]**
Renumbers lines in program starting at line n in increments of m. Default for m and n is 10.
Example: RENUMBER 100, 20 will give lines 100, 120, 140 ...

**RUN**
Causes program execution having first cleared all variables except the resident integer variables.

**SAVE s**
Saves program s on to cassette or disc. Filename up to 10 letters or numbers on cassette or up to 7 using disc. Filename must start with a letter.
Example: SAVE "PROGO1"

## 2.2 GENERAL COMMANDS

**DATA e1, e2,....**
Allows data to be given in a program (see READ).

**DEF**
Starts a definition of procedure or a function. Must be placed after main program, i.e. after END statement (see FN and PROC).

**DIM V [$] (n[,m])**
Reserves storage space for an array V. Numeric [or string] array of n rows [and m columns]. Multidimensional arrays are possible. Note zeroth element in rows and columns. DIM statement inserts zeros in numeric arrays and spaces in string arrays.
Example: DIM B(10) reserves storage for 11 elements in numeric list.
DIM A$ (3, 5) reserves storage for 4 rows and 6 columns of strings.
DIM NAME$ (10, 20), AGE (10,20), C$(12).

**ELSE**
Part of IF .. THEN .. ELSE structure (see IF)

**END**
Informs computer of end of program (optional).

**ENDPROC**
Indicates the end of a procedure definition (see PROC).

**EVAL(s)**
Enables user to enter a mathematical expression into a running program. The equation is put in a string and EVAL works out its value.
Example:
10 A$ = "A*X∧ 2+B*X+C"
100 z = EVAL (A$)

**FN**
Defines string or numeric function. Function always produces a result. Function may contain LOCAL variables and parameters may be passed to the function from main program (see PROC). End of a multiple-line definition ends with an = sign. A function appears after END of program.
Examples:
100 PRINT FNA(10)
290 END
300 DEF FNA(X) = X^2+4*X+5
is a one-line function definition.
In main program obtain value (line 100).
10 INPUT X
20 PRINT "FACTORIAL = "; FNF (X) (result)
30 END
40 DEF FNF(N)
50 Y = 1
60 FOR K = 1 TO N function
70 Y = K*Y definition
80 NEXT K
90 = Y

**FOR V = n to m [STEP p]**
Initialises a FOR .. NEXT loop. If STEP is omitted 1 is assumed. Nested loops allow up to 10 nestings.
Example:
10 FOR X = 20 TO 40 STEP 5
20 PRINT X
30 NEXT X
[20 (initial value), 25, 30, 35, 40 (final value)]

**GOSUB n**
Transfers control to subroutine at line n. The RETURN command signifies the end of the subroutine and transfers control back to the line following the GOSUB call.
Example:

```
100 GOSUB 1000
110
...
990 STOP
1000 REM SUBROUTINE
1010 ...
1100 RETURN
```

Do *not* enter subroutine except through a GOSUB call (hence line 990).

**GOTO n**

Transfers program to the line specified.
Example: 100 GOTO 50
Can also be used as a command to start a program without destroying values of variables.
Example: GOTO 50

**IF e THEN** < >

Sets up a test condition (or conditions) which controls subsequent actions.

**IF e THEN n**

If condition is true the command following the THEN is executed; if *not* control passed to the next line.
Example: IF X = 0 THEN PRINT "ZERO"
IF X>5 OR X<10 THEN 500

**IF e THEN** <> **ELSE** <>

In this case if condition is true everything after THEN and before ELSE is executed and if *not* true only statements after ELSE.
Example: IF X = 0 THEN PRINT "ZERO"
ELSE PRINT "NON-ZERO"

**LET**

Assigns value to variable (optional).
Examples: LET X = 6 can be written X = 6
LET A$ = "NAME" can be written A$ = "NAME".

**LOCAL**

States variables local to a function or procedure (see FN and PROC).

**NEXT [V]**

Terminates FOR.. NEXT loop (see FOR).

**ON NV (GOTO) n, m, p....**
**(GOSUB)**

Allows several possible transfers of control to a line (or a subroutine) depending on the value of NV.

Examples:
ON X GOTO 100, 200, 300 will cause control to move to line 100 (X = 1), line 200 (X = 2) or line 300 (X = 3).
ON AGE GOSUB 1000, 2000 transfers to subroutine at line 1000 (AGE = 1) or subroutine at line 2000 (AGE = 2).

**ON ERROR (GOTO) n**
**(GOSUB)**

Is used to trap an error by moving to line (or subroutine) which contains program section dealing with error.

**ON ERROR OFF**

Allows computer to deal with errors again (i.e. cancels effect of ON ERROR GOTO).

**PROC**

Calls a procedure from the main program.

**Procedures**

All procedures are placed after the END statement of the main program. All procedures are called from the main program by PROCNAME where NAME is the name given to the procedure. The beginning of a procedure is indicated by the statement DEF PROCNAME and the end by the statement ENDPROC.

**Formal parameters**

May be passed from the main program to a procedure by using

PROCNAME (A,B$) call line in main program

and

DEF PROCNAME (alpha, beta$) first line in procedure.

(i.e. A → alpha, B → beta).

**Global variables**

Are known to the whole program (i.e. main program and procedure).

**Local variables**

Are known only to the procedure and must be declared using LOCAL (C,D$). This ensures they have no affect on variables in main program.

Example: 100 PROCEXAMPLE (A,B$)

```
....                                    main program
1000 END
1100 DEF PROCEXAMPLE (alpha,beta$)
1200 LOCAL (C,D$)                       procedure
....
1500 ENDPROC
```

**READ V1 [$], V2 [$],...**
Allows insertion of data into numeric and string variables. Essential data is in correct sequence and form (i.e. string, numeric or integer).
Example:
10 READ A$,B,C,D%
....
900 DATA "SMITH", 3·5, 2·6, 25 puts "SMITH" into A$, 3·5 into B, 2·6 into C and 25 into D% (see also RESTORE).

**REM**
Computer ignores anything written in a line after this statement. Used to put remarks and comments into program.
Example: REM**SUBROUTINE FOR NAMES**

**REPEAT**
Initialises a REPEAT.. UNTIL loop. The computer repeatedly executes a set of instructions until a specified condition is satisfied. May be nested up to a depth of 20
Example:

| | |
|---|---|
| 10 N = 1 | |
| 20 REPEAT | initialise loop |
| 30 Y = N ↑ 3 | |
| 40 PRINT N,Y | body of loop |
| 50 N = N + 1 | |
| 60 UNTIL Y >999 | terminating condition |

**RESTORE [n]**
Resets data pointer to any selected line number.
Examples:
100 RESTORE sets data pointer to first data item in the program.
200 RESTORE 500 resets data pointer to that in line 500.

**RETURN**
Terminates a subroutine and returns control to the line following the GOSUB call (see GOSUB).

**STEP**
Increment (or decrement) of variable in FOR .. NEXT loop (see FOR).

**STOP**
Interrupts a running program.

**THEN**
Part of IF.. THEN construction (see IF).

**TIME**
Reads or sets internal timer. The timer counts in 1/100

second intervals. BREAK does not reset clock, CTRL BREAK does. Example:

10 TIME = 0

.. . . . .

200 PRINT TIME

**TO**

Part of FOR.. NEXT loop initialising statement (see FOR).

**UNTIL**

Gives condition for the termination of a REPEAT .. UNTIL loop (see REPEAT).

**:**

Separates multiple statements on line.
Example: 10 FOR N = 1 TO 10 : PRINT N*N : NEXT N

## 2.3 GRAPHICS, TEXT AND COLOUR

**Graphics screen**

Each point on the screen is represented by co-ordinates (X,Y) where X is horizontal value and Y the vertical value. Origin (0,0) is at bottom left.
Top right of screen is (1279,1023).

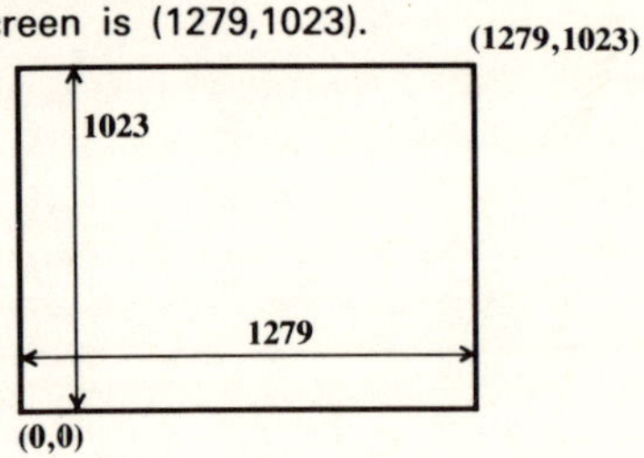


**Text screen**

Depends on mode (see MODE summary). Origin is top left of screen. Screen consists of characters across and lines down.
In normal use (MODE 7) there are 25 lines of 40 characters (see diagram).

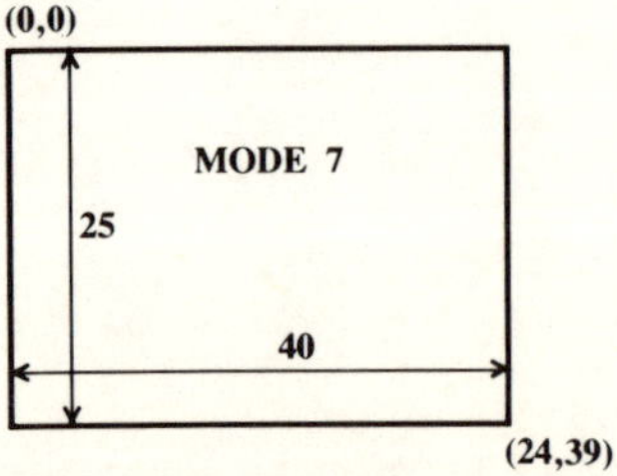

**CLG**
Clears graphics area. Moves graphics cursor to graphics origin of current graphics area [VDU 16].

**CLS**
Clears text area of screen. Text cursor moved to text origin of current text area [VDU 12].

**COLOUR n**
Changes text colour either to the foreground colour (n = 0 → 15) or the background colour (128 + n).

**Colours available**
*[Foreground numbers given, add 128 for background]*

*Mode 2*
0 black
1 red
2 green
3 yellow
4 blue
5 magenta
6 cyan
7 white
8 flashing black-white
9 flashing red-cyan
10 flashing green-magenta
11 flashing yellow-blue
12 flashing blue-yellow
13 flashing magenta-green
14 flashing cyan-red
15 flashing white-black

*Mode 0, 3, 4, 6*
0 black
1 white

*Mode 1, 5*
0 black
1 red
2 yellow
3 white

Can change colour by using VDU 19, n, m, 0, 0, 0 where n = logical colour and m = actual colour.
Example: VDU 19, 5, 2, 0, 0, 0 sets logical colour 5 to green.

**DRAW X,Y**
Draws a line from a previously specified point to the point (X,Y) in the foreground colour.
Example:
```
10 MOVE 20, 30
20 DRAW 100, 200
```
would draw line from (20, 30) to (100,200) [see also PLOT].

**GCOL n,m**
Sets colour for graphics [VDU 18]
n specifies mode of action
m specifies logical colour

n = 0 plot colour
n = 1 OR colour
n = 2 AND colour
n = 3 EOR colour
n = 4 invert colour
m (see COLOUR)
Foreground colour m
Background colour 128 + m

**MODE n**
Used to select display mode n = 0 → 7. You cannot change MODE within a procedure or function [see Summary of Modes].

**MOVE X,Y**
Moves the graphics cursor to the point (X,Y) without drawing a line.

**PLOT n, X,Y**
Generalised plot command; (X,Y) are co-ordinates on screen [VDU 25, n; X; Y;].
n = 0 *move relative*
n = 1 *line relative* in *foreground colour.*
n = 2 *line relative* in *logical inverse colour.*
n = 3 *line relative* in *background colour.*
n = 4 → 7 as above but *line absolute.*
n = 8 → 15 as 0 → 7 but *last point omitted* in 'inverting action'.
n = 16 → 23 as 0 → 7 but *dotted line.*
n = 24 → 31 as 0 → 7 but *dotted line* and *no last point.*
n = 64 → 71 as 0 → 7 but *single point plotted.*
n = 72 → 79 as 0 → 7 starting from (X,Y) search X axis both ways while pixels current background colour, points (X1,Y) and (X2,Y) set as points last visited, draw line between them.
n = 80 → 87 as 0 → 7 but plot and *fill triangle* made with previous two points.
n = 88 → 95 as 0 → 7 starting from (X,Y) search X axis right only until pixel is current background colour (X1,Y), then set as point most recently visited and (X,Y) as previous one, draw line between them.

**POINT (X,Y)**
Gives the logical colour at (X,Y) on screen. If point off screen it returns –1.

**POS**
Returns horizontal position of flashing cursor in current text window.
Example: X = POS

## VDU
Most useful graphics commands given below (see also VDU code summary).

VDU 29,X;Y;
resets graphics origin to (X,Y)

VDU 26
resets text and graphics cursors

VDU 5
joins text and graphics cursors.

VDU 24, Xl; Y1; X2; Y2;
defines graphics window (X1,Y1) bottom left and (X2,Y2) top right.

VDU 28, X1, Y1, X2, Y2
defines text window (X1,Y1) bottom left and (X2,Y2) top right.

VDU 30
moves text cursor to top left of text area.

VDU 31,X,Y
moves text cursor to (X,Y) of current text area.

VDU 23,1,0;0;0;0;
turns flashing cursor off.

VDU 23,1,1;0;0;0;
turns flashing cursor back on.

## VPOS
Returns vertical position of text cursor on screen.
Example: Y = VPOS

### Summary of Modes

| Mode | Colours | Machine | Graphics | Memory | Text |
|---|---|---|---|---|---|
| 0 | 2 | B | VHRG 640 × 256 | 20K | 80 × 32 |
| 1 | 4 | B | HRG 320 × 256 | 20K | 40 × 32 |
| 2 | 16 | B | MRG 160 × 256 | 20K | 20 × 32 |
| 3 | 2 | B | Text only | 16K | 80 × 25 |
| 4 | 2 | A,B | HRG 320 × 256 | 10K | 40 × 32 |
| 5 | 4 | A,B | MRG 150 × 256 | 10K | 20 × 32 |
| 6 | 2 | A,B | Text only | 8K | 40 × 25 |
| 7 | 16* | A,B | Teletext | 1K | 40 × 25 |

Modes 0 → 6 show the ASCII characters.
Mode 7 shows Teletext characters.
* Mode 7 requires different codes and statements for colour graphics from Modes 0 to 6.

At switch-on machine is in Mode 7.
In general Mode 7 is used for all applications where a full colour text display is required but no fine graphic detail.
In all screen modes that support graphics the range of (X,Y) values is X (horizontal) 0 to 1279 and Y (vertical) 0 to 1023.

| **KEYBOARD (Screen display Modes 0 to 6)** | **Screen display Mode 7** |
|---|---|
| ~ | ÷ |
| ^ | ↑ |
| ¦ | ‖ |
| \ | ½ |
| { | ¼ |
| [ | ← |
| } | ¾ |
| ] | → |
| Ø | 0 |

## VDU code summary

| No. | CTRL | Meaning | Alternative command |
|---|---|---|---|
| 1 | A | send next character to printer only | |
| 2 | B | turns printer on | |
| 3 | C | turns printer off | |
| 4 | D | write text at text cursor | |
| 5 | E | write text at graphics cursor | |
| 6 | F | enable VDU drivers | |
| 7 | G | make a short beep | |
| 8 | H | backspace cursor one character | |
| 9 | I | forward space cursor one character | |
| 10 | J | move cursor down one line | |
| 11 | K | move cursor up one line | |
| 12 | L | clear text area | CLS |
| 13 | M | move cursor to start of next line [in immediate mode RETURN] | RETURN |
| 14 | N | page mode on | |
| 15 | O | page mode off | |
| 16 | P | clear graphics area | CLG |
| 17 | Q | define text colour | COLOUR |
| 18 | R | define graphics colour | GCOL |
| 19 | S | define logical colour | |
| 20 | T | restore default logical colours | |
| 21 | U | disable VDU drivers or delete current line | |
| 22 | V | select screen mode | MODE |
| 23 | W | reprogram display character | |
| 24 | X | define graphics window | |
| 25 | Y | plot instruction | PLOT |
| 26 | Z | restore default windows | |
| 27 | [ | does nothing | |
| 28 | \ | define text window | |
| 29 | ] | define graphics origin | |
| 30 | ^ | home text cursor | |
| 31 | — | move text cursor to x,y | |
| 127 | | backspace and delete | DELETE |

## 2.4 SOUND

### ENVELOPE

Sets up pitch and amplitude envelopes in conjunction with SOUND statement.
Statement followed by 14 parameters: 6 parameters determine pitch envelope PI1,PI2, PI3, PN1, PN2, PN3
6 parameters determine amplitude envelope AA, AD, AS, AR, ALA, ALD
1 parameter specifies envelope number N
1 parameter determines duration of step in envelopes T
ENVELOPE N, T, PI1, PI2, PI3, PN1, PN2, PN3, AA, AD, AS, AR, ALA, ALD

| Parameter | Values | Function |
|---|---|---|
| N | 1 → 4 | envelope number |
| T | 1 → 127 | time of each step in 1/100s (bits 0-6) auto-repeat 0 or no-repeat 1 (bit 7) |
| PI1 | −128 → 127 | change in pitch (part 1) per step |
| PI2 | −128 → 127 | change in pitch (part 2) per step |
| PI3 | −128 → 127 | change in pitch (part 3) per step |
| PN1 | 0 → 255 | steps in part 1 |
| PN2 | 0 → 255 | steps in part 2 |
| PN3 | 0 → 255 | steps in part 3 |
| AA | −127 → 127 | change in amplitude per step (*attack*) |
| AD | −127 → 127 | change in amplitude per step (*decay*) |
| AS | −127 → 0 | change in amplitude per step (*sustain*) |
| AR | −127 → 0 | change in amplitude per step (*release*) |
| ALA | 0 → 126 | target level (*attack*) |
| ALD | 0 → 126 | target level (*decay*) |

**SOUND C,A,P,D** where
C = channel number (0 noise, 1→3 tone channels)
A = amplitude (−15 maximum amplitude, 0 silence) envelope control (1 → 16 selects envelope of same number)
P = pitch (0 →255, quarter semi-tone intervals, middle C 52)
D = duration (−1 continuous, 1 → 254 duration in 1/20 seconds)

Additional feature  C = &HSFN where
N = channel number (0 → 3)
F = flush control (0,1)
S = synchronization control (0 → 3)
H = continuation control (0,1)

## 2.5 NUMERIC AND TRIGONOMETRIC FUNCTIONS

**ABS(n)**
Absolute value of n (returns magnitude of number ignoring the sign).
Examples: ABS(6·2) gives 6·2, ABS(−6·3) gives 6·3.

**ACS(n)**
Arc-cosine of n. Gives angle in radians.

**ASN(n)**
Arc-sine of n. Gives angle in radians.

**ATN(n)**
Arc-tangent of n. Gives angle in radians.

**COS(n)**
Cosine of angle n. (n in radians)

**DEG(n)**
Converts angle n radians into degrees.
Example: DEG (PI/2) gives 90 (see RAD).

**DIV n**
Performs integer division
Example: 13 DIV 3 gives 4 (See MOD). [If a real number is used it is truncated i.e. 13·6 DIV 3·2 is as above]

**EXP(n)**
Exponential n, $e^n$.

**INT(n)**
Integer of n (rounds down)
Examples:
INT (2·6) gives 2
INT (−3·7) gives −4.

**LN(n)**
Natural logarithm of n, $\log_e$ n, ln n.

**LOG(n)**
Common logarithm of n, $\log_{10}$ n

**MOD n**
Gives remainder after integer division.
Example: 13 MOD 3 gives 1 (See DIV).

**PI**
Returns value of pi ($\pi$) i.e. 3·14159265

**RAD(n)**
Converts n degrees to radians.
Example: PRINT RAD (90) would return 1·57079633 (see DEG).

**RND**
Generates a random whole number between −2147483648 and + 2147483647.

**RND(n)**
Generates a random whole number between (and possibly including) 1 and n.
n = 1, generates random number between 0 and 0·999999

n = 0, repeats last random number given by RND(1).
n negative, gives value − n and resets random number generator based on n.
Example: RND (52) could be used for selecting one card from a pack.

**SGN(n)**
Determines whether n is positive, zero or negative. It returns
− 1 if n is negative
  0 if n is zero
+ 1 if n is positive

**SIN(n)**
Sine of angle n (n in radians).

**SQR(n)**
Square root of n. (Will produce error if n is negative)

**TAN(n)**
Tangent of angle n (n in radians).

## 2.6 INPUT/OUTPUT INSTRUCTIONS

**COUNT**
Counts all characters printed using PRINT command since last carriage return.
Example:

```
10 PRINT "HELLO"; COUNT
20 PRINT "BYE"; TAB(25); COUNT
30 PRINT COUNT
```

will give values 5, 25 and 0.

**GET**
Waits for key to be pressed and then returns ASCII value of that key. Used when waiting for a reply before continuing.
Example: X = GET will wait for key to be pressed and then put X equal to ASCII value of key.

**GET$**
Waits for key to be pressed and then returns string containing character of key pressed.
Example: A$ = GET$ will wait for key to be pressed and then set A$ equal to character.

**INKEY n**
*If n positive* waits n*1/100 second while constantly testing for key to be pressed (n = 0 to 32767). If key

pressed within time it gives ASCII value of key, if not pressed it gives − 1.
Example: X = INKEY (200) will test for 2 seconds. If key not pressed within that time it sets X − 1.
*If n negative* tests to see if a particular key is pressed (see Section 7).
Example: PRINT INKEY (− 102) would return −1 if the key M was pressed and 0 if not.

**INKEY$ n**
n positive. As for INKEY but returns key as character.

**INPUT V**
Allows data to be inserted in a running program.
Examples:
10 INPUT X, A$ allows input of a number and a string.
20 INPUT "type your age", A    prints out message in quotes and allows input of a number.

**INPUT LINE SV**
Will put in everything typed in (including spaces and commas) into a string variable.
Example: INPUT LINE A$

**Page mode**

| | |
|---|---|
| Enter page mode by pressing | CTRL N |
| Next page obtained by pressing | SHIFT |
| Leave page mode by pressing | CTRL O |

**PRINT Formatting**

**PRINT A**
Prints out value of numeric variable A.

**PRINT "YOUR NAME?"**
Prints out whatever is included within the quotes.

**PRINT**
leaves a blank line.

**PRINT A; B**
Causes printing of items immediately next to each other.

**PRINT A, B**
Causes next item to be printed in next print field. (Print fields are normally 10 characters wide.)

**PRINT A ' B**
Causes a new line to be printed at apostrophe.

**PRINT TAB(c); A**
Moves print c characters along line.

**PRINT TAB(X,Y); A**
Moves print to (X,Y) co-ordinate selected.

@% controls the overall field width, the total number of figures printed and the number of decimal places printed
@% = &B4B3B2B1 where
B4 determines string format
B3 selects format of number
B2 controls number of digits printed
B1 sets overall print width
B4 = 00 (default), 01 (strings formatted according to @ %)
B3 = 00 (General format), 01 (Exponent format), 02 (Fixed format)
[G format; integers printed as integers, 0·1 to 1 as 0·1 etc, < 0·1 uses E format]
E format; always prints numbers in scientific notation.
F format; prints numbers with a fixed number of decimal places, decimal points aligned vertically.]
B2 = 00 to 09 e.g. in F format specifies digits after decimal point.
B1 = 00 to FF field width in range 0 to 255.
Example @% = & 0002030C gives fixed format 3 decimal places and 12 character field width.

**Printer**

| | | |
|---|---|---|
| May be turned on using | CTRL | B |
| May be turned off using | CTRL | C |

**SPC (n)**
Allows printing of n spaces on screen (n = 1 to 255).
Example: PRINT "Name"; SPC(4); "Address" will put 4 spaces between Name and Address.

**TAB(n[,m])**
Moves text cursor to column n on line m.
Examples:
PRINT TAB(10); "HELLO" prints HELLO at column 10 on print line.
PRINT TAB(4,6); "BYE" prints BYE on line 6 starting at column 4.

**WIDTH n**
Sets the overall page width. Initially page width unlimited. Affects PRINT statements and output to printer.
Example: WIDTH 60 restricts line width to 60 characters.

## 2.7 STRING FUNCTIONS

**String**
Is a set of characters in quotes. ASCII code used to represent numbers in computer.
Examples: "SMITH", "PROG01", "*?!"

**String variable**
Is used to store strings. It consists of a set of characters followed by $ sign.
Examples:
NAME$, Z$, letter$
String variables can hold any number of characters between 0 and 255.

*Strings should be set to their maximum length the first time they are allocated to avoid wasting memory.*

**String array variable**
Is used to store an array of strings. A string array must be dimensioned (see DIM). Multidimensional string arrays are available. Subscripts run from 0.

**Substring**
Is any set of consecutive characters taken in sequence from the parent string.
Example: A$ = "COMPUTER", "PUT" is a substring.

**Concatenation**
Is the joining together of strings.
Example: A$ = "COMP", B$ = "UTER", A$ + B$ = "COMPUTER"

**String comparison**
May be done using any of the relational operators (see Section 2.8).

**String functions**

**ASC (s)**
Gives ASCII value of the first character in the string.
Example: ASC ("COMP") gives ASCII value of C which is 67.

**CHR$(n)**
Generates character associated with the ASCII value n.
Example: CHR$ (70) gives F.

**INSTR(s1, s2 [,n])**
Gives position of string s2 in string s1, the search being

started at the nth character. Default value on n zero. If no match then zero returned.
Examples:
X = INSTR("COMPUTER", "PUT", 2) will give X = 4
whereas
Y = INSTR("COMPUTER", "PUT", 6) will give Y = 0.

**LEFT$(s,n)**
Gives the n characters starting at the left hand end of the string s.
Example: LEFT$("HELLO", 2) will give "HE".

**LEN (s)**
Gives the number of characters in the string.
Example: X = LEN ("COMPUTER") will give X = 8.

**MID$(s, n, m)**
Selects part of string s starting at character n and continuing for a further m characters. If m omitted, continues to end of string.
Example: MID$("STRING", 2, 3) will give "TRI".

**RIGHT$(s, n)**
Gives the n characters finishing at the right hand end of the string.
Example: RIGHT$("WORDS", 2) will give "DS".

**STR$ (n)**
Converts a numeric expression into a string.
Example: STR$ (3·4) gives "3·4".

**STRING$(n, s)**
Results in a long string consisting of n copies of string s.
Example: STRING$(6, "ABC") will give "ABCABCABCAB-CABCABC".

**VAL (s)**
Converts a string which contains a number into a number.
Example: VAL ("3·4") will give 3·4 (see STR$).

## 2.8 ARITHMETIC AND LOGIC OPERATIONS

**Arithmetic operations**
\+ addition
− subtraction
* multiplication
/ division
↑ exponentiation
Example: 2↑3 = $2^3$ = 2×2×2 = 8

**Relational operators**

= equal to
< > not equal to
< less than
> greater than
< = less than or equal
> = greater than or equal

**Numbers**

*Real numbers* between $2 \times 10^{38}$ and $2 \times 10^{-39}$ are available and stored to 9 figure accuracy. Numbers smaller than $2 \times 10^{-39}$ are taken as zero.
Scientific (E) notation.
Examples:
1·73E5 = $1{\cdot}73 \times 10^{5}$ = 173000
2.56E−7 = $2{\cdot}56 \times 10^{-7}$ = ·000000256
*Integer numbers between − 2,147,483,648 and + 2,147,483,647 are stored with complete accuracy.*

**Variables**

*Real variables* may be represented by any set of characters provided (i) they start with a letter,
(ii) do *not* include spaces of quotes,
(iii) they do *not* start with a BASIC keyword.
Examples: AGE, HEIGHT are acceptable but LENGTH is not
letter, length, total are acceptable (since BASIC keywords are upper case).

**Integer variables**

Are distinguished by having a % sign after the last character.
Examples: A%, AREA%, count%
*Arithmetic calculations with integer variables are faster than with real variables but all numbers involved must be whole numbers.*

**Logical expressions**
**AND**

Combines relations so that [(condition 1) AND (condition 2)] is only TRUE when both conditions are true.
Example: IF X > 1 AND X < 10 THEN PRINT "BETWEEN 1 AND 10"
[also used as a bitwise operator for binary numbers (each number has 32 bits)].
Example:
85 AND 28 gives 20
85 is 24 zero bits then 0101 0101
28 is 24 zero bits then 0001 1100
85 AND 28 0001 0100 = 20

**EOR**
Combines relations so that (condition 1) EOR (condition 2) is TRUE when either (condition 1) or (condition 2) is true but *not* both.
Example: IF X = 0 EOR Y = 0 THEN PRINT "ONLY ONE OF THEM IS ZERO" [Also used as bitwise operator. Example: 85 EOR 28 gives 73.]

**FALSE**
Represented by the value 0 (binary number with 32 zeros).

**NOT**
Logically gives reverse of expression.
Example: IF NOT (A = B) THEN PRINT "NOT EQUAL"

**OR**
Combines relations so that (condition 1) OR (condition 2) is TRUE when either (condition 1) or (condition 2) is true or both are true.
Example: IF X > 0 OR Y > 0 THEN PRINT "ONE OR BOTH POSITIVE"
[Also used as bitwise operator. Example: 85 OR 28 gives 93.]

**TRUE**
Represented by the value − 1 (binary number of 32 ones).

**Order of precedence**

| | |
|---|---|
| Group 1 | (), functions, NOT |
| Group 2 | ↑ |
| Group 3 | *,/,DIV,MOD |
| Group 4 | +,− |
| Group 5 | =, < >, <, >, < =, > = |
| Group 6 | AND |
| Group 7 | OR, EOR |

## 2.9 FILE-HANDLING COMMANDS

**Data file**
Is a structured collection of data.
It consists of a set of *records* each of which contains several related items (*fields*) of information. The structure of each record in a particular file must be the same.
Example: A file consists of 2 records each of 3 fields.
SMITH, OXFORD, 10·65
JONES, BATH, 94·5
The field specification of each record is string, string, real numeric, i.e. A$, B$, C.

**File-name**
Is 7 characters maximum for disc and 10 characters maximum for tape.

**Channels**
Of communication between computer memory and permanent memory are 5 in number for disc and only 1 for cassette.

**File types**
Sequential access and random access available on disc but only sequential access on tape.

**Write to file**
Refers to transferring data from computer memory to permanent memory. (Output to file).

**Reading from a file**
Refers to transferring data from permanent memory to computer memory. (Input from file).

**BGET#NV**
Reads a single byte (character) from file.
Example: A = BGET#X reads single character from file on channel X and puts it into numeric variable A.

**BPUT#NV**
Writes a single byte (character) into file.
Example: BPUT#X, C will write character specified by variable C into file on channel X.

**CLOSE#NV**
Closes file.
Example: CLOSE#X closes file on channel X.

**EOF#NV**
Tests for the end of file (essential when reading from a file).
Example:
10 REPEAT
.....
30 UNTIL EOF#X
repeats loop until end of file on channel X.

**EXT# NV**
Gives length of specified file (disc only).
Example: PRINT EXT# X gives number of characters in file on channel X.

**INPUT#NV, V1, V2**
Reads a single record from specified file.
Example: INPUT#X, A$, B would read a record (consisting of a string and a real numeric) from file on channel X.

**OPENIN(s)**
Opens named file for reading.
Example: X = OPENIN(F$) opens file named F$ for reading on channel X.

**OPENOUT(s)**
Opens named file for writing (file creation).
Example: Y = OPENOUT (F$) opens file named F$ for writing on channel Y.
[N.B. If file already exists then it will be deleted and a new one created.]

**OPENUP (s)**
Opens file specified for updating. Example: Z = OPENUP (F$) associates file named F$ with channel Z (for reading or writing).

**PRINT#NV**
Writes a record into specified file.
Example: PRINT #X, A$, B would write a record (consisting of a string and real numeric) into file on channel X.

**PTR#NV**
Sets file-pointer to specified character (disc only).
Example: PTR # Y = 20 would set pointer to the 20th character in the file on channel Y.

## 2.10 MEMORY AND MACHINE CODE COMMANDS

**CALL**
Used to call a piece of machine code in a program.

**HIMEM**
Highest memory location BASIC uses for program and variables. May be altered to make room for machine code routines. It is the first memory location below the high resolution graphics memory area.

**LOMEM**
Gives address in memory above which the variables are stored. Normally LOMEM is set equal to TOP. Do *not* alter in the middle of a program.

**OPT**
Determines output produced on screen when assembly language routines are processed by the BASIC interpreter.

**PAGE**
Gives address in memory where BASIC has stored program. Usually set to the lowest available address in RAM but can be changed by the user.

**TOP**
Returns address of first free memory location above user's program.
Examples: PRINT (TOP-PAGE) will return memory needed for program itself.
As program is loaded instructions placed in memory locations above PAGE and TOP are adjusted appropriately. On running program variables are stored above LOMEM and return addresses below HIMEM. (Cannot change MODES within subroutine or procedure because this alters position of HIMEM.)
PRINT (HIMEM-TOP) indicates space remaining.

**Indirection operators**
? byte indirection operator (1 byte)
! word indirection operator (4 bytes)
$ string indirection operator (1 to 256 bytes)
Examples:
?45 refers to memory location 45.
?45 = 30 puts 30 into memory location 45 (equivalent to POKE).
PRINT?50 returns value in memory location 50 (equivalent to PEEK).
!a refers to memory addresses a, a+1, a+2, a+3 (most sig, byte).
$500 = "CATS" stores ASC11 values of C, A, T, S, RETURN in memory locations 500 to 504 respectively.

Memory addresses and contents specified in hexadecimal.
& means hexadecimal to follow.
~ gives hexadecimal value of decimal number.
Examples:
PRINT &FF gives 255
PRINT ~15 gives F

## 2.11 ERROR HANDLING

**ERL**
Gives the line number where the last error occurred.
Example: X = ERL

**ERR**
Gives the error number of the last error that occurred.
Example: Y = ERR

**ERROR**
Suppresses printing of an error message.
Example: ON ERROR GOTO 1000
[see also Section 2 ON].

**REPORT**
Prints the error message for the last error condition.

**TRACE**
Prints out line number of each line of program before execution.
Examples:
TRACE ON causes program trace.
TRACE OFF turns off trace (also ESCAPE or BREAK).
TRACE 1000 cause program trace for line numbers below 1000.

# 3 ERROR MESSAGES

| Error message | Error No. | Brief description |
|---|---|---|
| Accuracy lost | 23 | Loss of accuracy in calculating trigonometrical functions of very large angles. |
| Arguments | 31 | Too few or too many arguments for function or procedure. |
| Array | 14 | Array not known. |
| Bad Call | 30 | Procedure or function call incorrect. |
| Bad DIM | 10 | Array with negative number of elements. |
| Bad hex | 28 | Incorrect hexadecimal number. |
| Bad MODE | 25 | Attempt to change MODE in a procedure or insufficient memory for mode. |
| Bad Program | | Computer cannot follow program in memory. Start again. |
| Block? | 218 | Tape loading error. Rewind and play again. |

| Error message | Error No. | Brief description |
|---|---|---|
| Byte | 2 | Attempt in assembler to load a register with a number requiring more than 1 byte. |
| Can't match FOR | 33 | No FOR statement corresponding to a NEXT. |
| Channel | 222 | Cassette filing error, attempt to use channel which was not open. |
| Data? | 216 | Tape loading error. Rewind and play again. |
| DIM space | 11 | Insufficient storage to dimension array. |
| Division by zero | 18 | Attempt to divide by zero. |
| $ range | 8 | Attempt to put strings in zero page of memory. |
| Eof | 22 | End of file reached in cassette filing system. |
| Escape | 17 | ESCAPE key pressed. |
| EXP range | 24 | Cannot deal with EXP to powers greater than 88. |
| Failed at n | | On renumbering error found in GOTO or GOSUB statements. |
| File? | 219 | File name error found in cassette filing system. |
| FOR variable | 34 | Index variable of loop not numeric. |
| Header? | 217 | Tape loading error. Rewind and play again. |
| Index | 3 | Error in specifying index mode in assembler. |
| LINE space | | No room to insert line in program. |
| LOG range | 22 | Attempt to calculate LOG of a negative number. |
| Missing, | 5 | Missing comma in line. |
| Missing" | 9 | Missing quote in line. |
| Missing ) | 27 | Missing closing bracket. |
| Mistake | 4 | No sense in program line. |
| − ve root | 21 | Attempt to calculate square root of a negative number. |
| No GOSUB | 38 | RETURN without GOSUB |
| No FN | 7 | End of function without a function definition. |
| No FOR | 32 | NEXT without FOR. |
| No PROC | 13 | End of procedure but no procedure definition. |
| No REPEAT | 43 | UNTIL without REPEAT. |
| No room | 0 | All available memory used up. |

| Error message | Error No. | Brief description |
|---|---|---|
| No such FN/PROC | 29 | No definition corresponding to function or procedure call. |
| No such line | 41 | Line-number does not exist. |
| No such variable | 26 | Variable not assigned. |
| No TO | 36 | Missing TO in FOR statement. |
| Not LOCAL | 12 | Appearance of LOCAL outside procedure or function. |
| ON range | 40 | Incorrect X values (or too many) in ON X GOTO.. |
| ON syntax | 39 | Illegal ON.. GOTO statement. |
| Out of DATA | 42 | Attempt to READ more items of data than there were in DATA list. |
| Out of range | 1 | Branch out of range in assembler branch instruction. |
| Silly | | Incorrect RENUMBER or AUTO statements. |
| String too long | 19 | Attempt to have a string longer than 255 characters. |
| Subscript | 15 | Incorrect subscript for array. |
| Syntax | 220 | Cassette filing system indicates syntax error. |
| Syntax error | 16 | Incorrect command. |
| Too big | 20 | Too large a number (greater than $2 \times 10^{38}$). |
| Too many FORs | 35 | Attempt to nest too many FOR.. NEXT loops (maximum nesting 10). |
| Too many GOSUBs | 37 | Attempt to nest too many GOSUB.. RETURN subroutines (maximum nesting 26). |
| Too many REPEATs | 44 | Attempt to nest too many REPEAT..UNTIL loops (maximum nesting 20). |
| Type mismatch | 6 | Number expected and string presented or vice-versa. |

# MEMORY MAP

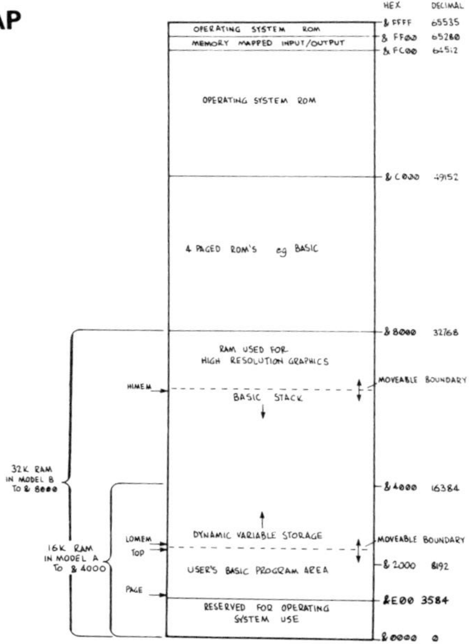


(detail)

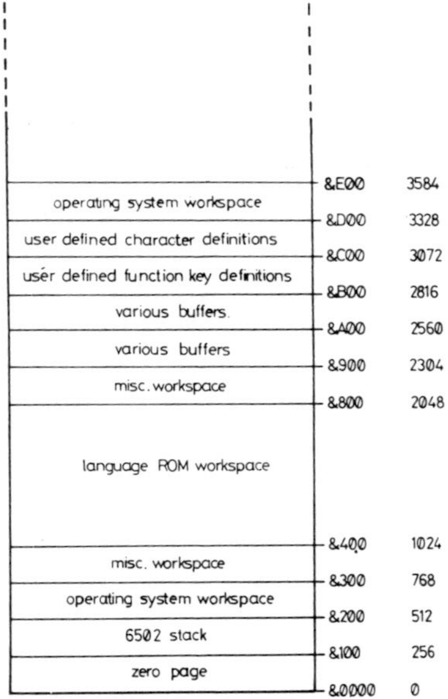

# 4 MEMORY MAP AND MEMORY MAP ASSIGNMENTS

**FF00- FFFF**
Operating System ROM

**FE00- FEFF**
Internal memory mapped input/output (SHEILA)

**FD00- FDFF**
External memory mapped input/output (JIM)

**FC00- FCFF**
External memory mapped input/output (FRED)

**C000- FBFF**
Operating system ROM

**8000- BFFF**
One or more languages ROMS (e.g. BASIC, PASCAL)

**4000 7FFF**
Optional RAM on Model B

**0000- 3FFF**
Always RAM

**E00**
Default setting of PAGE

**D80- DFF**
Allocated to machine operating system

**D00- D7F**
Used by NMI routines (e.g. by Disc or Econet filing systems)

**C00- CFF**
User-defined character definitions

**B00- BFF**
User-defined function key definitions

**A00- AFF**
RS423 receive, and cassette workspace

**900- 9FF**
RS423 transmit, cassette , sound and speech workspace

**800- 8FF**
Miscellaneous workspace

**400- 7FF**
Language ROM workspace

**300- 3FF**
Miscellaneous workspace

**200- 2FF**
Operating system workspace and indirection vectors

**100- 1FF**
**6502 stack**

**000- 0FF**
Zero page

## ZERO PAGE

**FF**
The top bit is set during an ESCAPE condition
**FD- FE**
Address following detected BRK instruction
**FC**
User IRQ routine save slot for register A
**D0 to FB**
Allocated to machine operating system
**B0 to CF**
Allocated to current filing system
**90 to AF**
Allocated to machine operating system
**70 to 8F**
Free for user routines
**0 to 6F**
BASIC language

# 5 OPERATING SYSTEM COMMANDS

| **Command** | **Meaning** | **Min abbr.** |
|---|---|---|
| *BASIC | selects BASIC ROM | *B. |
| *CAT | displays catalogue of files | *. |
| *CODE | allows user to incorporate his own command into operating system command table | *CO. |
| *DISC | selects disc file system | *D. |
| *EXEC | text files can be used as if they were keyboard input | *E. |
| *FX | OSBYTE calls may be performed directly from keyboard (see FX calls) | *F. |
| *HELP | prints version number of operating system | *H. |
| *KEY | programs user-defined keys (see section on keys and cursors) | *K. |
| *LINE | executes machine code at location pointed to by contents of USERV | *LI. |
| *LOAD | loads a section of memory | *L. |
| *MOTOR | turns cassette motor relay on and off | *M. |
| *NET | selects network file system | *N. |
| *OPT | For cassette and ROM filing systems<br>*OPT 0, 0 restores default values<br>*OPT 1, 0 turn of filing system messages etc. | *O. |
| *ROM | selects ROM file system | *RO. |
| *RUN | loads and executes a machine code program | */ |
| *SAVE | saves section of memory | *S. |
| *SPOOL | copies all screen output to a named file | *SP. |
| *TAPE | selects cassette filing system (1200 baud) | *T. |
| *TV | moves picture up and down screen<br>E.g. *TV255 moves display one line down | *TV |
| *¦ | ignored by computer (used to put remarks in a series of operating system commands) | *¦ |
| */ | treated as *RUN | */ |

[The command-line interpreter does *not* distinguish between upper and lower case characters in the command name.]

# 6 OPERATING SYSTEM CALLS

| **Routine** *Name* | *Address* | **Vector** *Name* | *Address* | **Summary of Function** |
|---|---|---|---|---|
| | | USERV | 200 | The user vector |
| | | BRKV | 202 | The BRK vector |
| | | IRQIV | 204 | Primary interrupt vector |
| | | IRQ2V | 206 | Unrecognised IRQ vector |
| OSCLI | FFF7 | CLIV | 208 | Command line interpreter |
| OSBYTE | FFF4 | BYTEV | 20A | *FX/OSBYTE call |
| OSWORD | FFF1 | WORDV | 20C | OSWORD call |
| OSWRCH | FFEE | WRCHV | 20E | Write character |
| OSNEWL | FFE7 | – | – | Write LF, CR to screen |
| OSASCI | FFE3 | – | – | Write character, &0D=LF |
| OSRDCH | FFE0 | RDCHV | 210 | Read character |
| OSFILE | FFDD | FILEV | 212 | Load/save file |
| OSARGS | FFDA | ARGSV | 214 | Load/save file data |
| OSBGET | FFD7 | BGETV | 216 | Get byte from file |
| OSBPUT | FFD4 | BPUTV | 218 | Put byte in file |
| OSGBPB | FFD1 | GBPBV | 21A | Multiple BPUT/BGET |
| OSFIND | FFCE | FINDV | 21C | Open or close file |
| | | FSCV | 21E | File system control entry |
| | | EVNTV | 220 | Event vector |
| | | UPTV | 222 | User print routine |
| | | NETV | 224 | Econet vector |
| | | VDUV | 226 | Unrecognised VDU commands |
| | | KEYV | 228 | Keyboard vector |
| | | INSV | 22A | Insert into buffer vector |
| | | REMV | 22C | Remove from buffer vector |
| | | CNPV | 22E | Count/purge buffer vector |
| | | IND1V | 230 | Spare vector |
| | | IND2V | 232 | Spare vector |
| | | IND3V | 234 | Spare vector |
| NVRDCH | FFCB | – | – | Non-vectored read character |
| NVWRCH | FFC8 | – | – | Non-vectored write character |
| GSREAD | FFC5 | – | – | Read char. from string |
| GSINIT | FFC2 | – | – | String input initialise |
| OSEVEN | FFBF | – | – | Generate an event |
| OSRDRM | FFB9 | – | – | Read byte in paged ROM |
| | | – | – | |

# 7 *FX AND OSBYTE CALL SUMMARY

| **Decimal** | **Hex** | **Function** |
|---|---|---|
| * 0 | 0 | Print operating system version number |
| * 1 | 1 | Reserved for application programs |
| * 2 | 2 | Select input device |
| * 3 | 3 | Select output device |
| * 4 | 4 | Enable/disable cursor edit keys |

| Decimal | Hex | Function |
|---|---|---|
| * 5 | 5 | Select printer type |
| * 6 | 6 | Set printer ignore character |
| * 7 | 7 | Set RS423 receive baud rate |
| * 8 | 8 | Set RS423 transmit baud rate |
| * 9 | 9 | Set flash period of first colour |
| * 10 | A | Set flash period of second colour |
| * 11 | B | Set auto-repeat delay |
| * 12 | C | Set auto-repeat period |
| * 13 | D | Disable various events |
| * 14 | E | Enable various events |
| * 15 | F | Flush all or just input buffer |
| * 16 | 10 | Select number of ADC channels |
| * 17 | 11 | Force start of conversion on ADC channel |
| * 18 | 12 | Reset user-defined function keys |
| * 19 | 13 | Wait for field synchronization |
| * 20 | 14 | Explode soft character RAM allocation |
| * 21 | 15 | Flush selected buffer |
| *124 | 7C | Reset ESCAPE flag |
| *125 | 7D | Set ESCAPE flag |
| *126 | 7E | Acknowledge detection of ESCAPE condition |
| *127 | 7F | Check end of file status |
| *128 | 80 | Read ADC channel/fire buttons/last conversion |
| *129 | 81 | Read key within time limit |
| *130 | 82 | Read machine high order address |
| *131 | 83 | Read top of operating system RAM address |
| *132 | 84 | Read bottom of display RAM address |
| *133 | 85 | Read lowest address for particular MODE |
| *134 | 86 | Read text cursor position |
| *135 | 87 | Read character at text cursor position |
| *136 | 88 | Reserved |
| *137 | 89 | Turn cassette motor ON/OFF |
| *138 | 8A | Insert character into keyboard buffer |
| *139 | 8B | Set file options |
| *140 | 8C | Select cassette file system and set speed |
| *141 | 8D | Reserved |
| *142 | 8E | Reserved |
| *143 | 8F | Reserved |
| *144 | 90 | Alter TV display position/interlace |
| *145 | 91 | Remove character from buffer |
| *146 | 92 | Read from I/O are FRED |
| *147 | 93 | Write to I/O area FRED |
| *148 | 94 | Read from I/O area JIM |
| *149 | 95 | Write to I/O area JIM |
| *150 | 96 | Read from I/O area SHEILA |
| *151 | 97 | Write to I/O area SHEILA |
| *224 | E0 | Cancel VDU queue |
| *225 | E1 | Set base number for function-key codes |
| *226 | E2 | Set base number for SHIFT function-key codes |
| *227 | E3 | Set base number for CTRL function-key codes |
| *228 | E4 | Set base number for SHIFT/CTRL function key codes |
| *229 | E5 | Escape = &1B |
| *230 | E6 | Enable/disable normal ESCAPE key action |
| *231 | E7 | Enable/disable user 6522 IRQ |
| *232 | E8 | Enable/disable 6850 ACIA IRQ |

# 8 DISC OPERATING SYSTEM COMMANDS

***ACCESS**
Prevents deletion of or writing to a file.
Example:
*ACCESS FILNAM L protects file FILNAM
*ACCESS FILNAM removes protection

***BACKUP**
Copies information from one disc onto another.
Example:
*ENABLE
*BACKUP 0 1
copies information on side 0 on to side 1

***BUILD**
Creates a file from the keyboard.
Example: *BUILD FILNAME

***CAT**
Displays catalogue.
Example: *CAT 0 (default current drive)

***COMPACT**
Puts spare space at end of disc.
Example: *COMPACT 1

***COPY**
Copies files from one disc to another.
Examples:
*COPY 0 1 FILNAME copies named file side 0 to side 1.
*COPY 0 1 L.* copies all files in directory L on side 0 to side 1.

***DELETE**
Removes single file.
Example: *DELETE MYPROG

***DESTROY**
Removes groups of files.
Example:
*ENABLE
*DESTROY *. M*
lists all files starting with the letter M and gives option to remove.

***DIR**
Sets up current directory.
Example: *DIR A

***DRIVE**
Sets current drive.
Example: *DRIVE 1

***DUMP**
Hexadecimal listing of file.
Example: *DUMP FILNAM

***ENABLE**
Necessary before *BACKUP or *DESTROY.

***EXEC**
Reads named file byte by byte.
Example: *EXEC GAME

***HELP**
Displays help file.
Examples: *HELP UTILS and *HELP DFS

***INFO**
Displays information about files.
Example: *INFO FILNAM

***LIB**
Sets library.
Example: *LIB:1.B sets library to directory B on drive 1.

***LIST**
Displays text file on screen with line numbers.
Example: *LIST DATA

***LOAD**
Reads named file into specified address.
Example: *LOAD FIL 2500

***OPT1**
Enables or disables message system.
Example: *OPT1 1 (enables)

***OPT4**
Changes auto-start option.
Example: *OPT4 1 will *LOAD the file!BOOT.

***RENAME**
Changes filename and directory.
Example: *RENAME OLD A. NEW changes filename OLD to NEW and changes directory from $ to A.

***RUN**
Runs machine code programs.
Example: *RUN PROG

***SAVE**
Copies specified section of memory on to disc.
Example: *SAVE "PROG" SSSS FFFF EEEE RRRR where SSSS = start address, FFFF = finish address, RRRR = reload address, EEEE = execution address.

***SPOOL**
Puts output to screen in a named file.
Example: *SPOOL PROG

***TITLE**
Changes disc title in current drive to 12 character name.
Example: *TITLE "SECRET INFO"

***TYPE**
Displays text file on screen without line numbers.
Example: *TYPE FILNAM

***WIPE**
Removes specified files, rearranges catalogue.
Example: *WIPE A.* deletes all files on current drive in directory A.

## 9 ASCII CODES AND KEY VALUES

SUMMARY OF ASCII CODES

| ASC11 | |
|---|---|
| 0 | nothing |
| 1 | next to printer |
| 2 | start printer |
| 3 | stop printer |
| 4 | separate cursors |
| 5 | join cursors |
| 6 | enable VDU |
| 7 | beep |
| 8 | back |
| 9 | forward |
| 10 | down |
| 11 | up |
| 12 | clear text |
| 13 | start of line |
| 14 | paged mode |
| 15 | scroll mode |
| 16 | clear graphics |
| 17 | define text colour |
| 18 | define graphics colour |
| 19 | define logical colours |
| 20 | default logical colours |
| 21 | disable VDU |

| | |
|---|---|
| 22 | select mode |
| 23 | reprogram characters |
| 24 | define graphics area |
| 25 | plot |
| 26 | default text and graphics areas |
| 27 | nothing |
| 28 | define text area |
| 29 | define graphics origin |
| 30 | move text cursor to 0,0 |
| 31 | move text cursor |
| 32-126 | characters (see Key Values Summary) |
| 127 | Back space and delete |
| 128-255 | Undefined Initially |

## KEY VALUES SUMMARY

| **Key Character** | **ASCII decimal** | **INKEY decimal** | **Key Character** | **ASCII decimal** | **INKEY decimal** |
|---|---|---|---|---|---|
| SPACE | 32 | −99 | B | 66 | −101 |
| ! | 33 | | C | 67 | −83 |
| " | 34 | | D | 68 | −51 |
| # | 35 | | E | 69 | −35 |
| $ | 36 | | F | 70 | −68 |
| % | 37 | | G | 71 | −84 |
| & | 38 | | H | 72 | −85 |
| ' | 39 | | I | 73 | −38 |
| ( | 40 | | J | 74 | −70 |
| ) | 41 | | K | 75 | −71 |
| * | 42 | | L | 76 | −87 |
| + | 43 | | M | 77 | −102 |
| , | 44 | −103 | N | 78 | −86 |
| - | 45 | −24 | O | 79 | −55 |
| . | 46 | −104 | P | 80 | −56 |
| / | 47 | −105 | Q | 81 | −17 |
| 0 | 48 | −40 | R | 82 | −52 |
| 1 | 49 | −49 | S | 83 | −82 |
| 2 | 50 | −50 | T | 84 | −36 |
| 3 | 51 | −18 | U | 85 | −54 |
| 4 | 52 | −19 | V | 86 | −100 |
| 5 | 53 | −20 | W | 87 | −34 |
| 6 | 54 | −53 | X | 88 | −67 |
| 7 | 55 | −37 | Y | 89 | −69 |
| 8 | 56 | −22 | Z | 90 | −98 |
| 9 | 57 | −39 | [ | 91 | −57 |
| : | 58 | −73 | \ | 92 | −121 |
| ; | 59 | −88 | ] | 93 | −89 |
| < | 60 | | ^ | 94 | −25 |
| = | 61 | | _ | 95 | −41 |
| > | 62 | | £ | 96 | |
| ? | 63 | | a | 97 | |
| @ | 64 | −72 | b | 98 | |
| A | 65 | −66 | c | 99 | |

| Key character | ASCII decimal | INKEY decimal |
|---|---|---|
| d | 100 | |
| e | 101 | |
| f | 102 | |
| g | 103 | |
| h | 104 | |
| i | 105 | |
| j | 106 | |
| k | 107 | |
| l | 108 | |
| m | 109 | |
| n | 110 | |
| o | 111 | |
| p | 112 | |
| q | 113 | |
| r | 114 | |
| s | 115 | |
| t | 116 | |
| u | 117 | |
| v | 118 | |
| w | 119 | |
| x | 120 | |
| y | 121 | |
| z | 122 | |
| { | 123 | |
| ¦ | 124 | |
| } | 125 | |
| ~ | 126 | |
| ESCAPE | | –113 |
| TAB | 9 | – 97 |
| CAPSLOCK | | – 65 |
| CTRL | | – 2 |
| SHIFT LOCK | | – 81 |
| SHIFT | | – 1 |
| DELETE | 127 | – 90 |
| COPY | | –106 |
| RETURN | 13 | – 74 |
| UP CURSOR | | – 58 |
| DOWN CURSOR | | – 42 |
| LEFT CURSOR | | – 26 |
| RIGHT CURSOR | | –122 |
| SPACE BAR | | – 99 |
| f0 | | – 33 |
| f1 | | –114 |
| f2 | | –115 |
| f3 | | –116 |
| f4 | | – 21 |
| f5 | | –117 |
| f6 | | –118 |
| f7 | | – 23 |
| f8 | | –119 |
| f9 | | –120 |